Dreams of My Heart

Aminath Neena

ISBN: 978-1-914130-09-0

Dreams of My Heart – Aminath Neena

OTHER TITLES FROM IMPSPIRED PUBLISHING

P.O.N.D – by John L Stanizzi

Stolen – by Candace Meredith

Stepping Up – By DC Diamondopolous

Pondering the Shoreline of Existence – By Ann Christine Tabaka

To my son Munzir, my daughter Hasna and to Fazy, with love

ACKNOWLEDGEMENTS

First and foremost, I am grateful to God Almighty for his enormous blessings on me without which I would not be capable of completing this prodigious milestone in my life.

Second, but no less crucial, I would like to thank Steve Cawte for his offer of publication at the very beginning, which undoubtedly helped me in building my confidence to pursue my dream.

Next, I owe a particular debt to Adrian David, fellow poet and writer, without whose encouragement and guidance, I would not have ventured into the task of unveiling my poems to an audience. Thank you so much Adrian.

My heartfelt thanks also goes to my English teacher Zahiya Zareer, whose approach to language teaching had been a colossal influence for my love for the English Language.

I must also thank Dr. Rafique Farooqi, who had introduced me to the world of poetry, a decade and a half ago from which I had evolved into who I am today as a butterfly would metamorphose from a cocoon. Thank you.

Contents

STRAWBERRY SEAS

Come, my sweet
Leave the memories bitter- sweet

Let us travel through strawberry seas
Sparkling in dandelion mist
where bunches of peonies
dance behind barriers of lust

of which, I shall pluck in thousands
while inhaling their heady scent
to weave fragrant garlands
as dainty tokens, to represent

of them doe - eyed slushy dreams
on which you and I shall float
all through the night as light beams
till we reach the castle we had sought

Never mind the in-between twist
of all yester years in this cosmic disc
As we counted life's humdrum bucket list
The new today beckons us to take the risk

Come my sweet-
It is time for us to meet-

DREAM CATCHER

First published at impspired.com on December 1ˢᵗ 2020

My love, your soul's being such a geek,
Oh! rather prudish and unruly tonight
he is making me utterly insomniac
by playing a game of hide and seek

He whispers my name so mellow
just as I try closing my laden eyes
and my heart starts searching for you
only to find an estranged pillow

Do something for me, my inamorato,
take him back inside you and subdue
then fly over to me across the seas
come back in a one-piece tuxedo

Or perhaps if you cannot be fair
eyes closed drift off into the clouds
then gently tiptoe into my dream
and just let me catch you there

CRAVINGS

That these amatory arms
be wrapped
around those mannish shoulders,
sometime soon,
in actuality;
Dare I dream?

That these doting lips
could trail a path
over those impassioned lashes,
sometime soon,
in actuality;
Dare I dream?

That these enamored fingers
should ruffle those
raunchy locks,
sometime soon,
in actuality;
Dare I dream?

That these sultry wisps of breath
be fused
with those blazing rasps,
sometime soon,
in actuality;

Dare I dream?

That these worshiping eyes
be locked within the pulpit
of those liquid abysses,
sometime soon,
in actuality;
Dare I dream?

That these raven tresses
held that face captive
within a cocoon of love,
sometime soon,
in actuality;
Dare I dream?

That these dreams of mine
were echoes of your heart
and these cravings do come true,
sometime soon,
in actuality;
Dare I believe?

WORDS

I

can feel

the love in your eyes

clearly without novice

Reflecting

the smile of spring blossoms,

pink tulips gazing

right across the dawn of my iris

Illuminating the glassy lake beyond

in mystic colors

of shades of orange and scarlet

of sunlit bliss

Dreams of My Heart – Aminath Neena

Boring into a fathomless pit

exploring bit by bit

travelling into valleys and hills

way beyond sweet chestnut and coppice

Demanding

to know the secret

of musk roses hiding beneath

thousands of sweet liquorice

Setting my soul ablaze by a force

beyond expression

that possesses my inner being

with an epic promise

And so with this seal,

no WORDS

are voiced at all,

by choice

MY OWN STAR

Love had bespangled me one night
in a lucid dream, rising high up superficially
As a shimmering armoured knight,
A lone star had gazed at me adoringly
Blinking now and then quite off beat
as so in rhythm with my dispatched heart beat

I thought he looked rather ghostly for a star
and began to inquire about his well being
When lamenting his melancholic memoir
I felt him whisper to me like a mortal being
He was quite the orphan- just like me
and grief- echoed in his vocabulary

I could feel him touch a part of me
invisible to this vitriolic cosmos mould
Kept away in a sacred sanctuary
like an unsung chansonette on hold
And as his shimmering light ran through my veins
my turbid blood ignited loosening the reins

Smiling at me, ever so handsomely
he had directly aimed his glow from up there
It seeped from the window sill alluringly,
dispatching kisses on my bed; on my pillows everywhere
It had followed my spread-out curves
its translucent beams electrifying my nerves

It was on my arms, my bosom; my bare skin
seeping through my hair; my tenderness as a whole
Silver rays blazing as gloss on my lips; on my chin
He had penetrated deep, deep into my soul
All the while my desire danced with his cosmic flame
till it all became synchronized to a single name

Stay together; we did till the stir of the orange ball
from the eastern horizon as another light
Then he had kissed me goodbye to commence his fall
promising to rise again at the tip of twilight
Though it was only a vision, I have no sorrow whatsoever
for surely twilight will rise someday; to stay forever.

AN EXOTIC FLOWER

First published at Journey of the Heart on January 6th 2021

I could paint the most exquisite rose

From the gentle stroke of my mind,

As the beautiful face of my mother

My thoughts flashing as silver ripples

to glisten on my liquified lashes

When I recall and remember

Her magical glow of rose pink,

a glittering beacon in a light house

Guiding my steps among all weather

Ever glowing -ever warming

Always beside me as my shadow

Helping me mould, holding her finger

Regardless of unpredictable seasons

Dreams of My Heart – Aminath Neena

Her sweet fragrance still lingers

rejuvenating my soul with such vigour

Just like it did as I lay within her unborn

a fountain of unconditional love, she was

that makes my heart flutter

Caressing the rough patches through the years

with her sweet nectar for sustenance

She was my partner, my soul sister

Her petals one by one had lifted me up

every time I fell, brushing the dust

gathered on my earthly cover

Till one fatal twist of fate

Forcibly separated the chord

That wove our souls together

Dispersing its shattered shreds

With the silent gust, as such is the theme

of this ramshackle journey's demeanor

And finally, with one deep breath

Feeble hands clasped in mine

She gave me, her last petal of flower

Like all flowers in this abode,

A rose, had bloomed to wither

Hush now, my sweet, it is time to rest- forever

SLEEPING WITH THE ENEMY

A facade of solitary bliss

through a beaming smile

was her placard of anguish

where pain resonated

gushing in between the fibrous tissue

as a flowing glacier that evaporated

through the ventricles

reverberating the psychotic laughter

smudging the walls in scarlet tentacles

eroding the surface shape

to assist in injecting the sugary venom

and as repulsive memories escape

reminiscing the times twin buds had to swallow

the poison- while nestled within the chalice

of the drunken enemy- sharing a pillow

dispatching the cancerous roots

of slime and molten lava-

And although their disgusting fruits

are long forgotten and lacerated

With the talons of the mundane time

And the organ has been castrated

to implant the effulgent beams

for a new life where hope grows a flower

in the graveyard of broken dreams-

the scars still bleed from time to time and remain

wishful remnants of a broken vase

a secret within the chambered domain

and to the outside world all the while

she was just another normal everyday face

topped with a dazzling glorious smile

THE LIFE OF ME

How do I remove thee

from my ludicrous heart

when 'tis not only

in that berserk muscle

that dwelt thee joyfully

but in candid, runs rampant

as a wild mustang, thee

In my virgin veins;

reigning scarlet seeps, thee

As for all that who dost cared

shalt surely foresee

So, tell me how I separate

thy essence forcefully

even in a thousand season's hours

when thou, simply is the life of me?

THE BLUES

First published at Academy of the heart and mind on 26th January 2021

I met my eyes

last night in a dream

and I saw it liquefied and streaming

with blue tears.

"Stop! Please stop right now" I urged.

"How can I? It's your heart that provokes me.

said my eyes, with downcast wet lashes.

"Don't you blame me now!"

"How am I supposed to control you?"

Quibbled a tiny voice from my chest.

So, I held them both captive in my hands

And firmly badgered both

of them imbeciles.

"Will you please listen to me

and stop this bickering?"

"Do you really want me to?" coaxed my heart.

"Don't you think it is better for you

to let it flow out?" said my eyes.

"At least that should

make you feel lighter!" echoed both.

And I woke up, sobbing.

I LOVE YOU

Did I ever tell you
that the world has waned
to a pair of soft liquid eyes
That reflects my most wanton sighs

Did I ever tell you
That the world has waned
to the charm of honey coated lips
destined to flutter on dewy bewitched sips

Did I ever tell you
that the world has waned
to a silver crested breast
on which these silky curls would take rest

Did I ever tell you
that the world has waned
to a seemingly dimpled chin
that could trample across territories forbidden.

Did I ever tell you
that the world has waned
to a muscle that beats to a combined rhythm
which resonates to my desired algorithm

Did I ever tell you
that the world has waned
to a timeless place of rainbow hue
from which reverberates the words, I love you

ODE TO A SCENTED BLOOM
First published at impspired.com on December 1st 2020

Oh jasmine; oh, my grace,
Thy softness and silky finesse
Thy flawless beauty, so enchants me
Aye, this meek psyche is baffled by thee

Me thinks thou belong with the sylphs
Thou confront no scuffle to those nymphs
Of the land, the rose so charming
The wild hibiscus so daring

Thy noble purity captures my heart
that no magic can reel it apart
And thy nectar- thy scent is the sweetest flow
Oh, my ladyship! And do they truly know?

'Tis the chastity in SHE not the flare
That matters so, nor the outside glare
Alas! those that seek the truth can but see
With eyes that seek beauty can only see

the hidden allure of the woman so feminine-
in the kosher elegance of thee, my jasmine

SCARLET DREAMS

First published at impspired.com on December 1st 2020

Scarlet dreams
Knitted in gold thread
Is what I conceal
Within bashful sighs
In the shelter of my eyes

Within closed lids
Sometimes I become a magnolia in bloom
My quivering petals wiping away your gloom
My fragrance fiddling with your senses
The essence disarming your defenses

Within silent lids
Sometimes I become a nymph of the seas
Singing enchanted melodies
That you may fall asleep buried in the soft swerves
Of my sea crusted feminine curves

Within cascading lids
Sometimes I appear as the encrypted moon
Fading away the dark clouds of rainy monsoon
That I may cast off the darkness of your ethereal base
My light gleaming over your face

Within half closed lids
Sometimes I arrive greeting you
As glorious morning dew
Applying dawn fresh-nature's balm

Dreams of My Heart – Aminath Neena

Seducing you with my soothing charm

But all this I do in scarlet dreams
of knitted gold thread
Secretly enclosed
Within bashful sighs
In the shelter of my eyes

IN PARADISE
*first published at spill words .com on 27th September 2020

Come,
Let me take you
Light years
Away in time
To the night
When our souls met
For the first time
Beside the milky lake
Of Eden
In paradise
Where beauty existed
Without envy
When time elapsed
Within a gust
Of the softest zephyr
When the silky petals
Of roses echoed
The song in our hearts
And when their nectar poured
As raindrops
Whispering a promise
Of a life time
Which, still brings shivers
To this edifice
Of melting femme,
Firing bolts of
Seasonal passion fruits
To haunt its corridors
From time to time,
And remember,
That same night,
I believed
In the divination
Of Love

SOUL MATES
*first published at spill words .com on 17th November 2020

Remember the night
before the harvest,
when the phantom of love lowered
its vessels to collect
The shine less
blue Sapphires and bloodless rubies
From twisted wobbly hearts
and fathomless murky depths
To replace
the shingles
with glittering diamonds
bathed in ambrosia
The night
when the moon craned
its neck for a glimpse
down below
In miracle land
And as the wind chimes danced
in rhythm
with the rose bud's song
and pink petals melted
In ecstasy,
That night
We
were born
again
and they, named us,
Soul mates

ONLY A DREAM

First published at Trouvaille Review on 31ˢᵗ October 2020

Diving into boundless depths
Embedded in a pair of gems
Pocketed on his moony lens
I once had this dream

Of a shower of jasmine
Falling over ebony tresses
Of Persian silk dresses
Spread on damask carpets

Of milky waterfalls
And the whispering breeze
Blowing over the trees
Carrying jeweled roses

Of silver trinkets engraved
On a golden pamphlet
Of flaming scarlet
Etched on bridal palms

And quenched thirsts
From sweetened sherbet
Of a dancing trumpet
Mimicking symphonic blues

Of brown teddy bears
Dancing with wind chimes
And painted nursery rhymes
Chanted as love songs

Of carved sculptures

Dreams of My Heart – Aminath Neena

adorned with ancient embroidery
mixed with antique calligraphy
As timeless mementos

On the mantelpiece
Then he blinked
his amnesia triumphed
Ruining everything

And it all vanished
Into a deep abyssal hem
Of lucid Freudian REM
And destiny woke me up

THE RENDEZVOUS
*first published at Trouvaille Review on 10th October 2020

The mystic and the child
Had a mysterious rendezvous
Once upon a luminous night
With the jigsaw of life to construe

Said the child to her elder,
'Kind sire, tell me please of this duress
Why do disappointments occur
Even at the threshold of success

Should we blame it on destiny
Or should we dwell it on imperfection? '
Pointing heavenward towards the canopy
Replied the humble person,

'Do you not see those stars smiling, my child
Glittering diamonds high up asunder
And occasionally by the clouds overcast they hide
Then, they shimmer yet one shade brighter

For if not for those clouds, man would fail to perceive
The significance of their own existence
As absence of blessings makes the heart retrieve
Glad tidings with more persistence

And patience had cured many a heart in pain.'
Just then, a tear drop flew from the little one's eyes
And as they both watched, it fell as rain
From the seemingly distant cloudless skies

A POET AND HIS WORDS

Tonight, you are my bespoke poet,
I am your words and the world is just ours
To make this a night of a thousand hours
together we will write a novel sonnet

Come, my heart, read me through your acronyms
when I place my semantics on them
Compose me with your poetic state of rem
when I reach closer with more synonyms

Bathe in my never-ending verbal musk
Drowning in the husky flow
As I bask in your poetic glow
till dawn's silver rises from gold of dusk

Pour out your ravenous beating heart now
I am waiting- feeling your heart racing
Listening to its rhythmic beat - I am breathing
Kindle my flammable words, to allow

the sparks of Collins and Webster to unite in flames
And together we can yield new vocabulary
to brighten all the pages of your anthology
so to keep the poetic fire burning with more rhymes

I have been dreaming of this glorious night
ever since the very beginning of my life
The time of wish fulfilment so rife
of literature, meeting with a literary knight

The world will remember the first time ever

when a poet - and his words, wrote their destiny
And so, our names will be engraved in history
Timeless- perhaps much more than forever

THE PLEDGE

'Tis a night of epiphany
whence forth, I make thee a pledge
Across the celestial galaxy
a solemn promise, I make

And so 'tis the naked truth-laden
dipped within the crimson froth
a promise I make, Oh, gentle moon maiden
By the honour of my vigilant jugular

Thou whom dwelt in the stoical ambiance
Smiling high above yonder
Shining with such nuptial radiance
Be mine sole witness this night

This pledge I dost make on this night
So long as this opaque muscle of mine
Flutters a single beat forthright
My beloved, I shall not part with thee,

Thus, this heart 's tenacity shall not ever
blither such like the ephemeral waves
stealing soft kisses that untimely waver
From the Ocean floor as he crusades

Wetting hers doting white sandy lips
from time to time so for more, she begs
to caress the shore with his luscious sips
Her cravings to fall on deafened ears

'Tis an ironclad pact I make thither
such a rumination for the ponder
Though this casket lump of flesh may wither
by the fragrant roses of a spring morn

Till this journey's non-exuberant end
My love will never cease hither
Grow'st from the evergreen pods that transcend
From the subaqueous part of my soul

Across a goodly length of time's ticking widow
these lovesick eyes of mine seek thy tender face
Upon a wee glimpse of thy bewitching shadow
overflows my jubilant wonder stream

Oh, how I love thee, my so beloved
By the occasional drizzle softly touching my lips
Inflaming husky temptations wayward
And the sizzling eucalyptus burning musky embers

Carved within the ring of the eternal one
At this whimsical hour, by my troth
By the mystical depths of the quaint woman
Henceforth this solemn pledge I dost make

To love and honour thee for infinity
Oh! patient messenger reigning yonder
Thenceforth hither I bequeath my destiny
So be mine witness this rapturous night

A MATTER OF TIME

I asked a flower, once
Do you miss the dew drops
that graze your cheeks
At the tip of dawn's silence?
Yes, I do, she whispers
But I know that I shall be grazed again, very soon
It's just a matter of time.

I asked once, from the ripple
of the flowing brook
Do you miss the fishes
that on your toes do tickle?
Yes, I do, she whispers
But I know that I will be tickled again, very soon
It's just a matter of time.

I asked the passing breeze, a while ago
Do you miss the rain drops
That hold you in his arms
While doing the occasional tango?
Yes, I do, she whispers
But I know that I shall be held again, very soon
It's just a matter of time.

I asked my heart, just now
Do you miss the one
Who touched you for the first-
and the last time, somehow?
Yes, I do, it whispered
But I know that I will be touched again, very soon
It's just a matter of time

MY MERCIFUL HEART

Those eyes, they tell me tales that speak f'r themselves/
in a language that which the likes of them stars speak
and so, does the flower gnomes and the ocean elves
whilst - those actions bid to me otherwise as bleak

Shall I perceive thee from my own merciful heart's rind
that which smiles flirting at thee nonchalantly/
and ignore the wrath of my own relentless mind
where time hath scyth'd and hath left its mark bluntly?

Should I not conceal these desires of mine temporarily?
Hast I to submit my woman's glory to defy this fate/
And risk the woe of being disillusion'd momentarily?
Shall I not but allow things to fadge at their crown state?

Nay, surrender I shall not! Nay me in a thousand tempest
years
f'r such bravery in the name of love is music, only for the
fool's ears

ODE TO A FLORAL DREAM

**First published at open doors poetry magazine on December 1st
2020**

Oh Fuchsia!
Thou who bring the summer's song
to autumn's crispy ears
Neither the pink gloss of camellia
Nor the satin gown of dahlia
Doeth pave justice
To thy magnum opus charisma

Oh Fuchsia!
Thou who bring the summer's song
to autumn's crispy ears
Gentle friend of midsummer begonia
Companion of summer blue lobelia
Thy demure belittles the aura
And dazzle of all seasonal forsythia

Oh Fuchsia!
Thou who bring the summer's song
to autumn's crispy ears
Curled velvet of Petunia
violet lips of glazed ambrosia
Thy bloom lone canst suffice
To the homosapien heart's dystopia

Oh Fuchsia!
Thou who bring the summer's song
to autumn's crispy ears

Pentamerous petals of peachy freesia
Clutching onto shades of sun kissed zinnia
Thy sultry pout hath shamed
many a lovers' wanton euphoria

Oh Fuchsia!
Thou who bring the summer's song
to autumn's crispy ears
My earthly floral Isabella
Wearing thy autumny tinted penumbra
Dreamt have I so for mine espousal chemise
Thy beauty smiling in a roseate veiled tiara

Fuchsia! Oh Fuchsia!
I beg thee; let not this be
one ficklest dream of utopia

HOME

If home is where we belong to un-roam
Then, let me show thee where mine 'tis home
Inscribed on thy forehead I see mine home
In thy fathomless eyes I see mine home
Sealed in thy wanderlust lips is mine home
Encrypted on thy silhouette is mine home
In betwixt thy wanton arms is mine home
Hanging to thy lullabying voice I cometh home
When I feel thou gaze me I cometh home
When I hear thou name me I cometh home
When I durst thee a glance I cometh home
Where ever thou art yon shalt be mine home
Hence, the gentlefolk doeth say, home's wrought
And cajoled forth to wherefore thy heart's sought.

GRACE

Oh, noble creature of the humankind

Art not thou an angel viewed as folly?

Here I dwell in the sea of melancholy

And there remain thou ever so loyal

To the ringed gunk that binds thee

When vows of many a common folk

Hath with time bled, ripped and broke

Yet thy regal heart cannot but withdraw

From the pleasures of smitten love

Applaud I do to thy bona fide candour

A salute for fine grace and noble valour

Even so, when my vexed heart weeps

DYSTOPIA

**First featured on BBC radio's "words and music" programme, on
21st Jan 2018**

I took a journey once
to the land of the learned dunce
Upon a blood -red sky
along which grief stood by
Where east and west met
across nautical boundaries set
Amidst a chest of cocaine truffle
Behind a steamy cauldron shuffle
Shaded by ancient druids
Deceived by sherbet fluids
Beyond chambers muffled with sounds
Of falsehood mimed among cahoots
Behind the altar of the puppet fleet
There, crushed as petals under feet,
Were the smiles of innocence
Stamped on each- a badge of impotence
Where a mass of intestines piped
Forming the ghettos blatantly hyped
Where walls of despair stretched
Across pools of blood drenched
Whilst woven tales fathomed
Among deaf tongues interlocked
Behind the altar of the puppet fleet

There, crushed as petals under feet,
Were the echoes of smiling innocence
Stamped on each- a badge of impotence
Where the bridge of humanity
lay tattered in garments of atrocity
There the gleaming silver of blades
Flashed upon trespassing clans
And when the boisterous shadows
Of their wolf pack herd narrows
Falling across fears of my past
I wake up with tears in my heart
diagnosed with a dose of myopia
On the road straight-to Dystopia

THE HOMECOMING

Arriving as the nimbus is my sovereign
Humble scion of water and air that reign

Pulse racing, eyes blazing; I welcome thee
For thy homecoming brings such wondrous glee
Mesmerized every time by thy glorious alchemy
Willingly I submit to thy passion in symphony
As a moth is fated to burn to a lamp's whim
My cumulonimbus, thou fill my heart to the brim
Through the eyes of the magnificent Venus,
I watch thee embrace my foliage, libidinous
Kissing my tender petals like glowing gems
Thy cool breath embalming my slender stems
Passing as shock waves to the roots buried within me
As I enfold my tendrils over thy neck lovingly
Clasping extra tight with a deep-rooted sigh
Thy drip drops of mirth whirls my feet to sway high
Reverberating in thy enchanting rhythmic dance
My tender pollen forms a wonder stream in a trance
Sometimes overflowing onto the musky sleeping rivers
Bringing such euphoria to my heart that it shivers
Thus, the fruit of our love- Our very own petrichor
Culminates this union- sealing our love forever more

Oh! What magnanimous joy thou bring to me
My prince, my loving companion of destiny

A SINGLE ROSE

A sunflower once inquired

from her neighbor

A single rose,

'Why is that my friend,

that you keep your petals folded

as a shield around you

when the bees swarm around

aching for their provision,

Don't you want to be admired,

adored and worshipped

like the rest of us?

Replied the rose, to her question

'I wait for a single bee

Dreams of My Heart – Aminath Neena

from all the creation

since the time of my birth

till the time of my death

I shall wait for him'

'Pardon me ma'am

But, Isn't that foolish....

Won't you wither away

with the cold winds of winter

and the harsh summer's sun? '

insisted her nosey neighbor,

The rose smiled

with tears in her eyes,

'You see, it's the way

I was created,
only for a single bee

and immune to the rest

who flutter around

though some have scratched my petals
Over time,

In their frustration

and burned in their own

Initiated, devastation

I shall stay fresh as long as I remain closed

My nectar and sweetness

providing me nourishment

deep within

If I open up

Even a single bit,

Before it's the right time

my nectar will dissipate

Into the winds

to be replaced by a poison

from which, my heart will wither

and tell me, my friend,

What good

Is

a flower

adorned with the brightest hue

on the outside

but, with a withered heart

devoid of nectar

to any roaming insect

For that matter? '

Upon hearing this confession,

Her neighbor

bowed her head

and

hushed.

A NEW BEGINNING AT NOTTINGHAM CAMPUS

With the early birds, this morning
as I woke up for a new day's calling

The gleeful sun smiled
from far across the lake
while the fading moon smirked
from right above the haze

The picturesque hills far beyond
waved and beckoned to me
whispering a particular song
audible to my heart only

The sparkling trees hoisted
their jewels. -oh! rubies so graciously
and a crimson carpet was embedded
on the naked grass discreetly

The ground breathed my name
and my feet played music on little twigs
putting the snails on the walls to shame
Oh! such breathtaking joy beyond limits

A Xanadu greeted me this morning
As I woke up for a new day's calling

ONCE UPON A TIME

Yesterday, once again
I entered
through
the flood gates
into her past
of once upon a time

From
the depleted
framework
I entered
into the bedroom
of once upon a time

Shadows
on the eerie ceiling
danced with phantoms
of the young woman
who lived there
once upon a time.

The crimson
tattoos
on the faded carpet
must have been badges
that she held close
once upon a time

The ghostly walls
still held the chains
onto which she was
positioned

as a mannequin
once upon a time

Easing my physique
through the entrance
I turned back
Forever - and gently
closed the door
of, once upon a time

INSATIABLE DREAMS

She is the libretto to which his poetry
could not find a rhyme
Yet she was his sonnet

She is the mystery to which his sagacity
failed to produce a key
Yet she was his kismet

She is the tempo for which his symphony
could not compose a rhythm
yet she was his lyrics

She is the touchstone of his velocity
with which he failed to ploy
Yet she was his wings

She is the hyperbole for which his trenchancy
could not opt for a suitable satire
Yet she was his literature

She is the paper for which his destiny
had omitted to spare some ink
Yet she was in his past, present and future

She was his "wish upon a star" melody
As he was her good luck charm
And yet... his lips would never taste hers

A PROMISE

Promise me that one day
you will meet me at the portcullis of heaven
As I would- do you;
For life on this earth is not befitting enough to
attune to a love as noble as ours

Promise me that one day
you will woo me in the land of milk and honey
As I would -do you;
For this world has got no delights suitable enough to
ravish a love as exotic as ours

Promise me that one day
you will doll me up with blooms from Eden
As I would-do you;
For this lodging has not a single posy suitable enough to
embellish a love as unique as ours

Promise me that one day
you will kiss me and hold me all through forever land
As I would - do you;
For this dwelling has concealed all paths that could
seal a love as passionate as ours

Promise me that one day
you will make me your mate in blissful paradise
As I would - do you;
For then my love, seek guidance as I ask the Almighty
to sanctify this divine love of ours

MELTED

This morning

as I watched

the sweet edges

of smiling dawn

tiptoe into my room

as bright wedges

of sun kissed tangerine

blushing into shades

of blooming gardenias

dipped in lemon green

In the mystic glow

with their warmth on me-

to fall on my sleepy cheeks

my heart craved

for you to touch me

right at that moment

with such intensity

that had you been really there

I would have melted

in your arms, in ecstasy

THE VENUS WOMAN
First published at Journey of the Heart on December 18th 2020

A true Venus born of a bone arose
From the remnants of time- delicate as a rose
Yet immensely powerful when defeated/
Courageous and defiant as needed

A hidden mystery yet to be figured out, she was/
Dark and forbidden as a graveyard at times, she was/
Yet so smooth and inviting in luminous splendor
A valiant fighter to claim equality for her gender

An incandescent face often misunderstood during the day
Yet persistent to survive in the vast majestic milky way
Those narcissistic red kings at times tries to steal her light
Each time she stumbles but holds her composure in flight

The majestic star one day- reached Zion's mighty gate/
pleasing the guardians with the most exotic serenade/
For underneath her iron core was a heart of pure gold
unvalued and unseen by the egoistic man of this world

There, for her patience - a choice was offered as a bonus
To culminate to one brawny Hercules or remain as Venus
with an aphoristic voice answered she in absolute precision
"Without any doubt - I would still want to be a WOMAN"

HIS VOICE

His voice
that of gold lace
echoes, Yes! echoes
like a silky wave
ruffling her ears
telling wonderful tales
and she keeps staring
with opiate eyes
visibly
intoxicated
Oh! if only he knew
the ripples he
could maneuver
in her core
with just a simple
touch of his
voice!

Oblivious
to the semantics
Yet aware, so aware
Of every pitch and pit
Of rhythmic mix
Is she
Of those delightful fruit
infused

with his sweet breath
rising and falling
from the twin buds
Oh! If only he knew
the tantalizing hunger
he could create
in her whole being
with just a simple
touch of his
voice!

Bewitched is she
to such a degree
that she
is afraid, so afraid
to breathe,
lest he may stop
the sweet flow
of hollow conversation
Oh! If only he knew
the lingering desire
he could conceive
in her heart
with just a simple
touch of his
voice!

WAY TO A POET' S HEART

Let me invite you
for a dive
into my
flaming
erogenous
heart
where my emotions
are laid bare

Take
a plunge
into its creamy
satiny folds
of desire
to which none
could ever claim
a share

You can
flip through
the canvas
of my naked
thoughts
and read
page by page
at your leisure-

And nibble on
the juicy buds

Of my creative soul
and taste
it's different
artistic flavours
at your own
pleasure

Or perhaps
turn over
so that
I could pour out
into your
trembling heart-
the joie de vivre
of my lucid poetry

and fumble through
your mind filling
you with pages and pages
of delicious words
embroidered
with the
virgin silk
of my coquetry-

And I know that
you would never
forget the first time
I touched you with
the exquisite warmth
of my thoughts
and the ecstatic depth
of my words

A FOOL'S PARADISE

Says the dove to the red-eyed hunter
"I am off flying to a far-off land
I do not fear you anymore
For I have connoted my blunder

Of over estimating the power
of a mere mortal- dark as can be
when it is the Almighty who hold
the reins as the omnipotent master

For I am through with fear
When faith has taught me to overcome
All negative felonies of such like
No more torments to adhere

It is time for you to move over
For I never belonged to you anyhow
Even for a fathom of a second
Though my wings had pulled me over

So, trod on to find your own pasture
For life is too short to hold onto Deja-vu's
And hallucinate 'bout a fool's paradise
Let go and be at peace- my friend for never."

ODE TO A GEMSTONE

Oh Aquamarine, brightest star of my eye

Thou art not only my faithful companion

But thou surely art a brawny lad of the sky

Whose alchemic fire is as grand as the canyon

Thou art a gleeful fellow whom I can confide

my deepest and darkest of all secrets abide

Oh Aquamarine, priceless gemstone of March

Of which a day I was born in solitude

Luscious beauty of the greenish blue arch

Lying across many a boundary of multitude

Thy gleam, surely is a paragon of loveliness

Shimmering on my neck of satiny silkiness

Oh Aquamarine, opulent treasure of the mermaids

Thou must wake my sailor from his slumber

Sing thy sweet melody vibrant for all shades

As so to make this a night to remember

Dreams of My Heart – Aminath Neena

For thy enchantment has clearly been foretold

Since the time of ancient sages, behold

Oh Aquamarine, sensual messenger of love

Tonight, blow thy wisps of silver ambience

Soar above the rough tracks as the gentle dove

To make him smell of my special fragrance

As a reminder of the pleasures that for him await

Far above the raging oceans of the human delight

Oh Aquamarine, sweetest breath of my life

Take my soft kisses across the seas to him tonight

Amorous and unsanctioned with such jubilant rife

Breathe on this impassioned soul unto him to ignite

For my beloved, needs his treasures of feather light

As such a wandering traveller needs the sun for daylight

A CHILD WITH AN IMAGINATION

When I was a little girl

With plaited pony tails and all

And mamma's hand- made pillow

As an imaginary doll

To play with, all alone

For me, the colours of the rainbow

And all in between that follow

Used to be mysterious chimes

Oscillating between positive and negative vibes

Eyes closed, I create an imaginary world

A completely new fjord

Created below the precipice

Of the sea of emotions concealed

Because, a child with an imagination, that was me

When I close my eyes

Sometimes, I see yellow

Dreams of My Heart – Aminath Neena

And it brings one happy feeling

Joyful and rather mellow

Painting my whole day aglow

Yellow trumpet flowers and yellow ripe mangoes

Spring forth here and there in rows

The times I see the lightest of blues

It makes me think of sky hues

Blue seems royalty

With navy blue uniforms a specialty

So does my blue pinafore dress and a blue lagoon

Lingering away in my mind's cocoon

Well, a child with an imagination that was me

Whenever, I see dark blue

It makes me shiver all through

For I think of the dangers of the unknown sea

Where Pirates and hungry monsters haunt

Drowning, as one possible fear of torment

Many a times, when I see red

The boldest colour of the spectrum

Funny thing, I never think

Of reddish danger or blood curdling dread

But makes me think of wrapped up presents

For wish fulfillment

Red ribbons and red balloons

Of happiness and contentment

Yes, a child with an imagination that was me

At times when I see green

I feel unusually safe and serene

As if I have come home

The green grass and the green trees in our backyard

Green leaves of varying shape

Supporting the green fruits sour to taste

Play a part to relax my body and mind from within

When in those times, I see orange

I never associate it with fire or a fiery mould

No not me, not even for a second

Dreams of My Heart – Aminath Neena

But it does make me awfully hungry,

The reason a wee bit unknown

Perhaps orange sodas, sweets and lollypops, is my concern

For, a child with an imagination, that was me

At times when I see white

I think of the light

Of my sweet mother

A symbol of purity and chastity all together

Her white prayer veil and clean white laundry

And occasionally the white crescent in the national flag

Occupies my mind, yet another mystery

At those dark times, whenever I see black

The most dreaded colour to sight

I cannot help but think

Of the devil carrying a black sack

Of hideous sins to commit

And black witches roaming in the darkness of the mundane
night

Oh! A child with an imagination that was me

When at those times I see pink

My favourite of colours, till this day

I think of myself in pretty pink clothes

Not to mention, the pink flowers and pink frills of all sorts

For me, Pink powder puff and pink satin

All together makes the perfect woman

And finally, at those very rare moments when I see purple

A colour marvelously special

Gives me a feeling of mystery and excitement

And believe me, something physical

Stirs deep from my soul

Though I still was child at heart then

The strange feeling lingers on, quite magical

Surely, a child with an imagination that was me?

IN MY DREAMS

Let me embrace you to my dreams, dear heart,
For in there, we can be wide awake
Whilst the rest of the world hibernate
And there, no vallation we shall ever meet

There, measureless joy should be ours
Where I see you and you know me
For in our shared knowledge we can see
This waking life's concealed powers

There, neither you nor I have any questions
Nor do we need any validation or permission
For what we desire is right there without illusion
No feasibility for any ill-timed suggestions

There, only the truth we will speak
Where our tongues will have no constraint
And our limbs will meet no restraint
The language of the heart we shall keep

There, it is only love and laughter and fun
For in dreams we do get to fulfill our desires
The very ones that keep us awake for hours
So, come to me in my dreams, my dearest one

A LITTLE FAIRY

Sleeping so peacefully
Enveloped in soft folds blissfully
On my bosom, you smile
A perfect little angel
Carved expertly from my flesh
As a token of my love
With eyes as black as the night
You, my little fairy,
Are so beautiful to me

Oh, my scented gardenia!
A priceless gift you are
Of divine intervention
Bestowed on this mortal
by the munificent Almighty
My flowing tears subside
As forgotten rain clouds
With your adorable consistent chatter
Such a blessing you are on my platter!

Oh, my little tulip!
You are my heart's music
My soul's fulfillment
My mind's vitality
The laughter of my kindled spirit
The centre of my existence,
My anguished heart soars,
Doing somersaults at the sight
Of your bonbon face- so bright

Oh, my sweet child of May!
Forgive me if I fail in any way
to fulfill the role of both parents
For he has left us forever now
Swapping me the responsibility
And I am trying my utmost best
This, I hope you would understand
when you wear the crown of a mother
Perhaps in one score or another

Oh, my little rose bud!
Just like a bird nurtured and loved
One fine day you are sure to fly away
From the comfort of this tree
Where the fingers of my palm bled
While gathering the sticks
To light the fire that warmed your spirit
And you will make your own
One day, with your very own

Oh, my precious princess!
Till then, I shall love you-yes!
Within the natural confines
of my woman's potentiality
To nourish your growing heart
With the golden fruits of my soul
So that you will be a merit
Not only to a closed society
But to mankind, for eternity

So, sleep well my darling
In this warm nest, my fledgling
The curvature of my breasts
As your comforting blanket
Be safe in the knowledge
that in order to fill your heart
with the purest of joy and mirth
there is absolutely nothing at all
that I wouldn't do for you, my little doll

DARK MAGIC

You command your spirits
Crossing over the limits
To create impediments
In my path
So that my will may weaken
When night falls
With the carpet of darkness
To cover your evil deeds

You burn the voodoo dolls
to bring out ailments of all sorts
The doll you made in my shape
Using my stolen essence
So that my physic is vulnerable
And you can attack the spirit within
To possess my soul
Using your parchment of deer skin
And ink of saffron

You embark on the quest
of making charms in an amulet
Burying them under the sands
Of the tracks that I follow
So that my feet drags
Me to your cabin
In a dazed state
And you can catch me
Like a bird in your net

You try to meet my gaze as I walk
A daily victim of your stalk
wearing the sacred eyeliner
So that you can hypnotize me
And force me to love you
But this you never knew
That I am protected by a higher being
And you can never possess my heart
because I simply, am not in your destiny

HER AQUA PURA

That ambrosial
look
glazed
by those wanton
lashes
makes her think
of tasting
iced
aqua pura
under the shade
of green foliage
on a hot
scorching
summer
afternoon

That jeweled
voice
moving
in unison
with those
frolicsome lips
makes her recall
comforting
times
of juvenility
and
whimsical
flashbacks
that console
her marred heart

That lovey-dovey
face
sets her
heartbeat
a little faster
with topsy turvy
emotions
and reflects
the most
vehement
desires- which
she keeps
off limits
from the rest
of the world

SUBLIME BLISS

Standing across the bridge
gazing into an oblong ridge
of the deep mesmerizing kind
I am lost-
Lost within the musk

Of the soft brown steep
beneath the river so deep
wading through liquid fire
my heart ignites-
Ignites to pure lust

In the distance an enchanting melody
chants with our symphony
My feet slips
and I drown-
Drown ever so willingly

you so absolutely tantalize
expertly mesmerize
In chocolate candy frost
that I inhale-
Inhale the sweet remedy

of the green green grass
obscuring yester years grey grey canvas

brushing so tender against my heart
that I break apart-
Break apart from the kiss

The gliding stream is mine to luxuriate
together with the moon light's affiliate
Sharing my joy
and I start to cry-
Cry out in sublime bliss

Churning light sparks to flute
promising to conceive its radiant fruit
the essence of our love
Seems so intense-
Intense enough to defy

Every negative illusion
with such vibrant gratification
and all that is left-
Left Is just
An exalted deep s-i-g-h! ! ! !

SONG OF A WOMAN

May I

ponder

along your path

linger upon your warmth

lather you within my hearth

smother you with my saccharine breath

someday, in this lifetime?

Can I

trace a line

across pacified lips

paint a flower over mollified lids

cover you along in candy nips

shower you a bit with maple sips

someday in this life time?

Could I

enclose you

within my silky hold

enfold you with a loving mould

engrave you in my heart, in bold

embrace you, with my nuptial gold

someday in this life time?

Should I

scurry alongside you

as your best

entomb my head on your chest

make this my eternal quest

forget about just the rest

someday in this life time?

Would you mind

If I carefully,

picked your art

tenderly, loved you for a start

simply, bedazzled you apart

gently, touched your heart

someday in this life time?

Will you,

for once, belong to me

mind, heart and body

to be my one and only

so that I may smile in glee

to receive this heavenly decree

someday, in this life time?

GARDEN TALES

When a fragile *Arabian jasmine*
fell gracefully into the brawny arms
of a *night blooming jasmine,*
Oh! what a love story they brew

From the mingling of their incense!
Could it be another replica
Of agarwood and frankincense?
Or rosewood and woody myrrh?

Could their union be close
to a glaze of bourbon and vanilla?
Perhaps a mix of evening primrose
And jubilant juniper berries?

Was it an earthly enigma,
As the scent of freshly cut grass?
Or a heavenly charisma,
The fragrance of a *houri* in paradise?

So thought awestruck Mr. Wind
who was the hoodlum behind this episode
his wayward wanderlust to rescind
as he breathed in the floral bonne bouche

LIGHT A CANDLE

First published at Borderless Journal on October 14th 2020

You, light a candle in your heart

Fill your soul with the brightness of its entourage
Let not this world be a selfish mirage

Let them kill your roseate dreams
Ignore your poignant pleas
Squash your path in mud
Drench the innocent in blood

But you, light a candle in your heart

Fill your soul with the brightness of its entourage
Let not this world be a selfish mirage

Let them spill out the venom
Attack the one without any weapon
Destroy your precious homes
Ruin your auspicious hopes

But you, light a candle in your heart

Fill your soul with the brightness of its entourage
Let not this world be a selfish mirage

Let them smudge your garments

With their gratuitous comments

Let them do all the damage
While they can still rampage

But you, light a candle in your heart

Fill your soul with the brightness of its entourage
Let not this world be a selfish mirage

Let them create havoc in the land
But this you must understand
Surely you will overcome this phase
For, the oppressed move closest to God's space

Until then, light a candle in your heart

Fill your soul with the brightness of its entourage
Let not this world be a selfish mirage

And if not a candle, a tiny spark
Will definitely, drive away the darkness at large.

THE WOMAN- A NATION'S PRIDE

The gleam in her eloquent eyes
The allure of her succinct sighs
Black or White- Asian or Hispanic
Forever elegant and charismatic
The woman, she is never a stigma
For truly, she is a blessing- an enigma

The curvature of her swaying hips
The shimmer on her dewy lips
The ornateness of her demeanor
Her bearing, poise and grandeur
Her seductive smile is lethal
For she is just a magnificent oracle

The tenderness of her feminine touch
Her kindness and empathy as such
Her iconic plethora of healing
Her bionic sassiness and persevering
Her bosom is a bed of silkiness above
Surely, she is the symbol of love!

The clemency in her trusting heart-
Her goddess like patience- had ripped apart
The arrogance of many a hard-hearted soul
A homemaker or judge, she's played her role
A momma or stateswoman- she's done it all
For she is the ultimate glad-tiding of all

The delicacy of her candid chatter
The brilliance of her gray matter
Her innate vigilance and prudence

On the face of peril, her resilience
Her phenomenal scent of musk roses and vine
The woman, she is the elixir of life-divine

WEEDS

Weeds
whisper
unheard hellos
over
frolicking
meadows
beautiful mellows
in sunset yellows
green and purple
lamenting widows
later to form empty hollows
streaks of whites and blues
destined to disperse as echoes
their song of sorrows
unsung
and follows
new generations
of seeds in shadows

BLANK VERSE

My precious, I am a poem
Do you feel the unrhymed scheme of my heart
and the definite rhythm of its beat?
They decipher the syllables for you to comprehend
The mystery and the delicacy of me
And an indefinite amount
they must resemble
For I am a Blank Verse
Of the modern-era

Move your lips ; Read my lines
Do you hear the rhythm and meter of the iambs?
You may have to be a little patient
For some start with closed syllables
While the others are exposed and vulnerable
A set of five in total, they must be
One behind the other
Revealing, joy and woe
Loss and gain of yesteryears

Take a tumble ; Scrutinize my verses
For I need a thorough understanding
Have you noticed the metaphors and similes yet?
The alliterations and assonance
In them, do you see consonance?
Did you manage to capture the onomatopoeia?
They might be a little tricky though
For pain and suffering
Had words and exclamations somewhat confused

Dreams of My Heart – Aminath Neena

Take a deep breath ; Read me once again
Do not mind the hyperbole and oxymoron
They are just part of life
Learn to evade the allusions and the imagery
Even the rhetoric and the irony
If any trouble, in between the ride
Do repeat the last two lines
For they will give you the ALLEGORY
That you need to see most- - -in a POEM

THE LEAF

A leaf
Fell down
Gliding smoothly
A halo of a velvet crown
While his mother silently
Watched with teary eyes
And a numbed heart
Hushed with frozen sighs
As her soul was torn apart
By the abysmal wind
She could not bend
Her colossal rear
Nor could she lend
Her dress robe's coil
Still canvassed by fear
For the grip of the soil
Beneath held her captive
And even if she did manage to sway
The wind would be selective
And blow her precious, farther away
Clutching the dangling creepers overhead
She sobbed the song of a mother
"Stay safe where ever you may bred
In the eerie silence a ghostly whisper
"And may it be known one fine day
That the bosom that held you secure
Never did she cast you away
But held on till you were mature
Enough to battle the realities
Of life's miscalculations and pain

And was able to weigh the truth of follies
Even during a drizzle of rain
And this you must know for sure, my son
I never meant to abandon you
But rather, it was the wind that drove you into a run
And even then, I had tried to reach you
I had given you the blood
That runs freely in your veins
And I had given you the flood
That of which, at times will moisten your eyes
Because when I had nothing to offer you
On the final day of the tempest

I have gifted you -

With my tears, at its best"

THE GREAT TURNING POINT

THAT those monuments of love will someday be forsaken
Concrete and ashes cold and shaken
Who would have thought?

THAT east and west will someday pursue a common enemy
Meeker in size yet macabre as can be
Who would have thought?

THAT neither the princess nor the pauper will someday
matter
Each for their own to take heed or shatter
Who would have thought?

THAT those who held their heads high in defiance will
curtsy
Small and broken- forlorn and topsy turvy
Who would have thought?

THAT those dexterous cyborgs will someday form an
alliance
Seeking consolation from a mightier power than science
Who would have thought?

THAT the earth can do its magic the way it was meant to be
Altruistic and majestic, wild and free
Who would have thought?

THAT tossed in the deep sea, colourless will be mankind
With the tide, nowhere to go nowhere to mind
Who would have thought?

THAT some will perish still a number would be reborn in
sincerity
And they will resist and pray for a common cause in
solidarity
Who would have thought?

THAT they will relearn kindness and gain fulfillment
Through hardship and solitary confinement
Who would have thought?

THAT they will believe in healing and miracles- and of
epiphany
And with blessings from the skies will smile serendipity
Who would have thought?

THE BIRTH OF LOVE
First published in Spillsword on 13th Feb 2021

Once, on a halved lunar month
The moon,
vacillated in her steps
lost her path
and slipped behind

Quite miffed, the sun veiled his face
denouncing to disrobe her
of his paternal luminance

The earth saw her wandering
like a lost kitten
Dazzled by her simplicity
and unique beauty,

he rose from his earthly throne,
"Come, be the queen of my heart", he bowed
"But you already have a Queen
-And you have little ones
to symbolize your union", she mumbled
"She is just a matter of chance
and has little to do with my heart-

Otherwise, I might have died, a bachelor
devoid of off-spring-
to pass on my legacy"

The moon, charmed by his calibre
was at a loss for words
as well, lost her heart

Dreams of My Heart – Aminath Neena

smiling behind downcast lashes, she obliged
when the earth took her in his arms
the stars stopped twinkling and gazed
filled with wonder
shutting off their eyes

diminishing the rim
temporarily
giving the couple, complete solitude

The night lingered till an eternity
while the sacred flowers
bloomed at the altar of the galaxy

in unison, the heavens smiled
as their joined hearts
melted and poured into each other

and that significant night
from the union of the earth and the moon,
and their entwined souls,

Love, was born for the first time
to be certified in history.

and from that night,
till the end of time
their flame is rekindled
On every lunar eclipse.

MY MOTHERLAND

The beauty of splashing waves
Bespeak my homeland
Loving the stretch of white gold
Pure and innocent motherland

As the whimsical wind unties the pony tails
Of the lavish coconut palm
Whistling a song in her delicate ears
The song of freedom and calm

An heirloom from our forefathers
Echoes all the way across the Earth
Which, may hold a thousand splendor
Fiddle not with my heartstrings as worth

And as we awaken everyday
With the scent of the salty sea breeze
Let us all make a solemn pledge
Kindle a flame of salvation and peace

To stick together as the shoals of fish
Roaming in our deep seas
Make a prayer for unity and love
For generations to never cease

I love thee so much my mother
In you, my heart believes
And I am so proud of you
My Country- My Maldives

THE SUN, THE SEA AND ME

For miles and miles
Of turquoise emerald
No living being resides
Only us three assembled
I breathe in the balmy freshness
Of the tropical saline breeze
Feel the silky subtle coolness
Of the seductive plethora beneath
It's ripples silently caressing
Circling my torso, sending shivers
Like a lover gently coaxing
"Stay! Don't leave just yet", whispers
And for hours WE sway together
Making memories to last forever

THE SILVER BUTTERFLY

Do you still remember or ponder about
That silver butterfly with wings of cheese blue
With a stick full of breadfruit sap, as glue
The one, in spring you chased all around?

I can still recall your surprise
When I had gained its trust
And wiping my hands of its powdery dust
I gave it to you gently as a prize

Though I never told you how I had it
so calm and composed within my fist,
I will do so as this year's 'New Year gift'
When we celebrate of love- three decades of it

Well dear, it so happened in a trot
That while I sat day dreaming
Under the guava tree counting
the petals of daisies, for love and love not

That silvery angel came and sat on my ringlets
Right down my cheek it was moving
straight into my heart it was aiming
For a while it tickled as I ignored the bets

When it sat on my ring finger
I saw its sweetness clearly
And then I knew instantly
Without a single streak of waver

Dreams of My Heart – Aminath Neena

Why you yearned for it so much
So, without so much of a hesitation
As it fluttered its wings in frustration
And - though it was as sweet as blueberry fudge

I caught it in my hand again
and simply gave it to you so
I only had a little of its dust and no more
preferring my loss for your gain

But then I still wonder today, *ma cherie*
Whether, then I did the right thing
as it seems that it was only a passing fling
For you have found your "*mon cheri*"

And I do wonder where that butterfly is now
Perhaps roaming just like me- high up above?

THE LOTUS

Growing in the deep wilderness
Amongst dozens of succulent buds
Bloomed a single white lotus
Her habitat, a glassy lake in the ruins
A traveller passing by
was captivated by her unique elegance
"I would be humbled if mademoiselle
would take refuge in my garden
for I shall build a magnificent pond
and nurture you like no other
With my gentle caresses I shall
transform you into an eternal bloom
and make you an immortal being
making sure that you never collapsed
with the violent hurdles of life's raging tempest"

Folding her delicate petals inward
The lotus whispered, in velvet lace
"I neither want immortality nor do I
need an impressive environment
I only need your love and affection
and your heart's undivided attention
For I know that before me, many such flowers
would have bloomed in your garden
and withered away, without your knowledge
content I am in this lake and will be,
so please good sire, do let a poor girl be"

Dreams of My Heart – Aminath Neena

Deeply affected by her refined manner
Change himself to a hermit, he did
and built him a dome, in the ruins
to become the caretaker of the lake

To this day, he still remains,

Staring at the single white lotus
Among dozens of succulent buds
Growing in the deep wilderness

BEYOND BARRIERS

If imagination
was a graceful bird
I would
imagine
that I had
turned
into one that soars
higher and higher
with the smiling clouds
travel across
boundaries
till I could reach you
and sit next to you
singing sappy love songs
to make you happy

If thoughts
were pretty flowers
I would
think
that I had
blossomed
into a sassy rose
whose fragrance is carried
across the seven seas
with the floating breeze
to reach your
nostrils
and let you slumber

into blissful
dreamland

If dreams
were wishes
fulfilled
I would
dream
that I could
surpass
beyond invisible barriers
across the flimsy curtain
that separates us
to be right next to you
at this very moment
my eyes drinking you
my body warming you
and my heart loving you

THE PAINTING

Using my shuttle brush

With soothing touches

Let me paint your face

In colours of love blush

Let me first draw a line across

with my golden art

that has been dormant

amongst velvet gloss

I may trail a celestial ridge

Sprinkle my silver dust

Over hills and flourishing valleys

Crossing the aristocratic bridge

With violets and soft blues

I shall create a rainbow

Dreams of My Heart – Aminath Neena

to resuscitate a dream

of an enigma of pleasing hues

Let me smudge your cheeks in crimson sips

then, see me bring you alive

by scrolling my pencil down below

to trace the outline of your lips

Gently getting them to stir up

filling them with sappy tales of sugar cane

then coating with the shiny balm

Of honey comb and maple syrup

As a finishing touch, with one final stroke

I shall embalm your chiseled structure

In ancient ointments of rose essence

toned with juniper berries and chestnut oak

So that you will be mummified in art

and held as a willing prisoner

fully dipped in colours of my love

preserved as a painting in my heart

LOVE AUGUMENT

Like a river bursting
to flood with mirth
Like the clouds thirsting
to rain on mother earth
Some days her heart overflows
and needs a release of love
for her psyche over weighs
like the river and the clouds above
But where could she possibly drain
all her mused love augment?
How on earth would she act as rain?
What on earth would end her torment?
Should she empty it on the ocean sands?
Or should she pour it on the barren lands?
Could she sprinkle them as silver dust?
Or could she shower them as liquid luck?
Who should be spared?
And who should be reared?
Should she dare trespass on any?
When neither the ocean nor the land
belongs to her only?
Should she dare take a chance
When she could neither become dust
nor could she flow as liquid
even as a happenstance?

SOUL MATE

Once upon a lonely night
I looked at the sky
Illuminated with a million stars
And I thought I saw your portrait
Etched deeply in the blue parchment
with a spectrum of vivid colours

Once upon a grey morning
I looked at the damp grass
glistening with a thousand raindrops
and I thought I smelt your cologne
revitalizing my swaying senses
with the freshness of my unique one

Once upon a sunny afternoon
I looked at the sparkling sea
with the shimmering ripples swaying to and fro
and I thought I heard your voice
Whispering endearments in my ear
mixed with the gentle splashing waves

Once upon a misty evening
I looked at the blossoms in my garden
gleaming with the nectar that bees and butterflies ravish on
I thought I tasted your lips
with a pinch of honey dew and salt
rejuvenating my lustful impulses

Once upon a lifetime
I looked at the forlorn winding roads
with the faintest of breezes passing by
I thought I felt your touch on me
Gently filling me with anticipation
for the day we meet soul to soul and mould into one.

A PRETTY LADY

Raindrops are pretty so pretty
I shall catch you before you do me
Hopscotch and dance with maidenly glee-
Painting the luscious greenery- pretty so pretty

Replacing my sorrow, pretty so pretty
Washing everyone's tears in to the musty drains
Delighting the mirthless empty plains
Arriving as a sensual nymph - pretty so pretty

Praise be to the creator-pretty so pretty
Your footsteps sing such a melodious tempo
Frolicking with the seasonal monsoon tango
Humming like a sparkling fairy- pretty so pretty

Your vestments are pretty so pretty
Your docility incomparable to any-
Your enveloped buoyancy, a cure to so many-
My dainty lady, you are- pretty- so pretty

MEN OF HONOUR

Where have all the honourable men vanished to?
Were they all devoured by the Loch Ness monster?
For I see none here but chauvinistic barbarians all along
To derive pleasure in gaming with the fair sex

Where have all the honourable men vanished to?
Did they all disappear into the Bermuda Triangle?
For I see nothing here except for narcissism all along
That has nothing to offer to a deserving dame

Where have all the honourable men vanished to?
Were they all lured by the Pied Piper of Hamelin?
For I see nothing but juvenile gold diggers all along
Scheming to play 'Cinderella' in the modern fairy tale

Where have all the honourable men vanished to?
Did they all become ensnared within the remnants of
yesterday?
For I see none who would uphold chivalry's sword all along
No, there aren't any Prince Charming's left, anymore

Perhaps they are all taken by the goodly earth women
Ah! Such pitiful remorse- for the remaining unattached
women

BLEEDING HEART

Demons of my past drag me back
Into a deep isolated well in the ruins
Bleeding heart
claiming pervert

Deeper and deeper I fell into the bottomless pit
Filled with the scurrilous monsters
Disheveled hopes
Disoriented bones

Their foul breath against my face
Grotesque arms slithered on my body
Trampled mud
Crimson blood

Rapacious monsters demanded subjugation
While my soul cried out for renewal
Trembling lips
Shriveled limbs

A light was shining in the distance
Little veins in my heart longed to reach it
Dissolute fires
Solemn desires

The agony castigated my inner being
While the enemy soared in triumph
Dispatched screams
Tangled dreams

Faraway the light glowed and beckoned me
Slowly once more a futile attempt
Howling winds
Broken wings

The light flickered for a second
My eyes opened heavenward
Haunted castles
Fallen angels

A stifled moan escaped my throat
Silence engulfed the horrendous night
Deceptive disdain
Endless pain

HOPE

-A sestina poem

The night is sombre and gravely forlorn
And the candle we lit is almost burnt
Coughing its last breath is our flame
But with you beside me, I have hope
For beams of the waning moon in the darkness
Appear to me as tell-tale signs of daylight

So faraway may seem triumphal daylight
And the tranquil silence is so forlorn
But our love still glows in the darkness
Though our tattered lighthouse is visibly burnt
Up the creek without a paddle- yet we have hope
Even as the tempest shrieks and howls at our flame

As the current huffs and puffs to douse our flame
And water gushes in blocking the orb of daylight
Still, in these hours of macabre dread is- hope
The angel of death smiles perilous and forlorn
And on your shoulders as I lay broken and burnt
A gleaming beacon- is our love in the darkness

This abode will surely conquer the darkness
Though the ebbing light is all but a soothing flame
In this home of concrete bricks grey and burnt
But with the first swirl of jubilant daylight
Our love will weather away the storm so forlorn

So, what we have to live for now is only hope!

Full to the brim is this heart of mine, with hope
Though enveloped we are now, in total darkness
The culmination of faith will lift this blanket forlorn
With the strength of our love as a guiding flame
Even the erratic flash of molars reminds me of daylight
As the rodents devour the stale bread half- burnt

With forces adamant to leave our world fatally burnt
Yet, I have no fears lurking in the testament of hope
For victorious we will be with the rise of daylight
Despite hungry wolf packs traversing in the darkness
With you dear heart, as my eternal flame
We will surely overcome this tantrum forlorn

Ah! the burnt wax has caked again to abhor this darkness
Soon new HOPE will help to revitalize our flame
And at the tip of daylight, gone, gone will be times- forlorn

UNBRIDLED LOVE

His face
a mere festschrift
of her deepest
emotions unleashed
with strips of
disrobed imagination
stares at her
beneath the gossamer
of dreams embellished
as she floats towards him
in a state of hypnosis
with the soft breeze
playing melodies of jazz
with her heart strings
and when they meet,
undoubtedly famished
half way through
the glossary
of rose avenue,
their senses dismissed
the meager path
to relish on
fruity inhibitions
till finally they sealed
the epitome of
unbridled love.

About the Author

Aminath Neena is an English lecturer from the picturesque archipelago nation of the Maldives. An avid lover of words, poetry is a hobby closest to her heart. Her poems usually revolve around  themes such as love, relationships, spirituality, society, and global issues. According to her, poetry is the gateway to spirituality because it resonates purity like no other. Among her achievements include having her poem featured in 'Words and Music', a programme on BBC Radio. Her poems are published or forthcoming in a range of international platforms like the Trouvaille Review, Spillwords, Open Door Poetry Magazine, Fiddles & Scribbles, Impspired Magazine and Borderless Journal. Aminath holds an MA. in TESOL from the University of Nottingham. She believes her writings to be a reflection of her thoughts, her feelings and her life.

Made in the USA
Las Vegas, NV
13 August 2024